Primordial Strength Law Enforcement Training Volume 1
By Steven Helmicki

ISBN: 978-0-557-29451-0

This is dedicated to returning as many brave law enforcement personnel to their family's through intensive strength training and conditioning that allows them to face adversity with an extra layer of protection: Primordial Strength.

No task becomes too large for these capable men and women who risk their lives daily so that we may rest peacefully.

Train to Fight Crime and Survive. Period.

Pre-habilitation/ warm-up: Jump rope x 2 minutes; bent arm pullovers x 20 reps; shoulder internal/external rotation with mini-band x 15 reps; patella tendon tracking x 15 per leg (hard glute activation.)

Fasciae stretch: Place 8kg kettlebells in the rack, clean, front squat position and decend to maximum depth with arched back and perfect squat mechanics and sit for 30 seconds.

Move all weights dynamically, except for pre-hab movements which are to be performed slowly and methodically.

Phase L- train 3 times per week for 3 weeks. Maintain the same weights but improve speed and velocity of movements.

Workout 1

Kettlebell Front squats below parallel box 8kg x 3 immediately followed by 16kg x 3 repeat 3 times non-stop

Hydration

Band good mornings mini-band x 3 immediately followed by monster-mini band x 3 repeat 4 times non-stop

Hydration

Kettlebell farmers walk 12kg x 20 yards immediately followed by 24kg x 2 yards repeat 3 times non-stop

Hydration

Kettlebell shrugs 12kg x 3 immediately followed by 24kg x 3 repeat 3 times non-stop

Hydration

Chins bodyweight x 2 immediately followed by bodyweight plus 20lbs x 2 repeat 3 times non-stop

Hydration

Close grip incline bench 25% of 1rep max x 2 immediately followed by 40% of 1 rep max x 2 repeat 3 times non-stop

Hydration

Kettlebell swings 8kg x 2 immediately followed by 12kg x 2 repeat 3 times non-stop

Workout 2

12 inch step-up with 12kg kettlebells x 3 per leg immediately followed by 16kg x 3 per leg repeat 3 times non-stop

Hydration

Rope sled pulls hand over hand 50lbs x 10 yards immediately followed 100 lbs x 10 yards repeat 3 times non-stop

Hydration

Kettlebell shoulder press 8kg x 3 immediately followed by 12kg x 3 repeat 3 times non-stop

Hydration

Kettlebell curls 4kg x 3 immediately followed by 8kg x 3 repeat 4 times non-stop

Hydration

Band pushdowns light band x 5 immediately followed by average bands x 5 repeat 3 times non-stop

Hydration

Neck harness extension/flexion 15 reps x 2 sets

Hydration

Sport gripper x 3 immediately followed by trainer gripper x 3 repeat 4 times non-stop

Workout 3

Back squat empty bar x 2 immediately followed by 95lbs x 2 repeat 4 times non-stop

Hydration

Kettlebell deadlifts 12kg x 1 immediately followed by 16kg x 1 immediately followed by 24kg x 1 repeat 3 times non-stop

Hydration

Kettlebell bent rows 8kg x 2 immediately followed by 12kg x 2 immediately followed by 16kg x 2 repeat 3 times non-stop

Hydration

Dumbbell hammer curls 4kg x 2 immediately followed by 8kg x 2 repeat 4 times non-stop

Hydration

Sled drags forwards 75lbs x 10 yards immediately followed by 150lbs x 10 yards repeat 2 times non-stop

Hydration

Landmine twist 15lbs x 2 immediately followed by 30lbs x 2 repeat 3 times non-stop

Phase A- train 3 times per week for 3 weeks.

Workout 1-

Tire flip- 200lbs x 1 immediately followed by 300lbs x 1 repeat 3 times non-stop

Hydration

Landmine press 25lbs x 1 immediately followed by 50lbs x 1 repeat 3 times non-stop

Hydration

Sled rows 2 plates x 5 immediately followed by 4 plates x 5 repeat 2 times non-stop

Hydration

Sled curls 1 plate x 3 immediately followed by 2 plates x 3 repeat 3 times non-stop

Hydration

Close grip bench press bar x 5 immediately followed by 25% of 1 rep max x 5 immediately followed by 40% 1 rep max x 5 repeat 2 times non-stop

Hydration

Kettlebell swings 4kg x 2 immediately followed by 8kg x 2 immediately followed by 12kg x 2 repeat 3 times non-stop

Workout 2

Trap bar deadlift 95lbs x 2 immediately followed by 135lbs x 2 repeat 4 times non-stop

Hydration

12 inch Step ups 12kg kettlebells x 2 immediately followed by 16kg kettlebells x 2 repeat 3 times non-stop

Hydration

Flat bench 12kg kettlebells x 3 immediately followed by 24kg kettlebells x 3 repeat 3 times non-stop

Hydration

Band triceps pushdowns light x 3 immediately followed by average x 3 repeat 4 times non-stop

Hydration

Band curls light x 3 immediately followed by average x 3 repeat 4 times non-stop

Hydration

Kettlebell swings 4kg x 4 immediately followed by 8kg x 4 repeat 3 times non-stop

Workout 3

Close stance squat bar x 3 immediately followed by 95lbs x 3 repeat 3 times non-stop

Hydration

Kettlebell bent rows 4kg x 3 immediately followed by 8kg x 3 repeat 5 times non-stop

Hydration

Kettlebell shrugs 4kg x 4 immediately followed by 8kg x 4 immediately followed by 12kg x 4 repeat 5 times non-stop

Hydration

Neck harness flexion/extension 5 reps x 5 sets with 5 seconds rest

Phase W- train 3 times per week for 4 weeks.

Workout 1

Squat Bar x 25 reps

Bench bar x 25 reps

Bent row bar x 25 reps

Shrug bar x 25 reps

Straight bar curl x 25 reps

Lying triceps extension bar x 25 reps

Workout 2

Bodyweight vertical jumps on soft box 4 inch x 1 immediately followed by 6 inch x 1 repeat 3 times

Hydration

Medicine ball smashes 4 kg x 1 immediately followed by 8kg x 1 immediately followed by 12kg x 1 repeat 4 times

Hydration

Dumbbell Hammer curls 10lbs x 4 immediately followed by 15lbs x 4 immediately followed by 20lbs x 4 repeat 4 times non-stop

Hydration

Neck harness extension/flexion 5lbs x 5 immediately followed by 10lbs x 5 immediately followed by 15lbs x 5 repeat 3 times non-stop

Workout 3

Kettlebell front squats 4kg x 2 immediately followed by 8kg x 2 immediately followed by 12kg x 2 repeat 3 times non-stop

Hydration

Kettlebell clean and jerks 4kg x 2 immediately followed by 8kg x 2 repeat 4 times non-stop

Hydration

Kettlebell snatches 4kg x 2 immediately followed by 8kg x 2 repeat 4 times non-stop

Hydration

Sled push 90lbs x 12 yards immediately followed by 180lbs x 12 yards repeat 3 times non-stop

Hydration

Grippers: perform one rep with each gripper you are capable of closing and repeat from easiest to hardest 3 times

Phase P1- train 3 times per week for 4 weeks.

Workout 1

Kettlebell farmers walk 16kg x 10 yards immediately followed by 24kg x 10 yards immediately followed by 32kg x 10 yards repeat 2 times non-stop

Hydration

Kettlebell shrugs 16kg x 3 immediately followed by 24kg x 3 immediately followed by 32kg x 3 repeat 3 times non-stop

Hydration

Kettlebell deadlifts 16kg x 3 immediately followed by 24kg x 3 immediately followed by 32kg x 3 repeat 2 times non-stop

Hydration

10 yard sprints x 7 times non-stop walk back rest only

Workout 2

Barbell squat 65lbs x 2 immediately followed by 130lbs x 2 repeat 4 times non-stop

Hydration

Land mine press 15lbs x 2 immediately followed by 30lbs x 2 immediately followed by 45lbs x 2 repeat 2 times non-stop

Hydration

Barbell bent rows 65lbs x 3 immediately followed by 100 lbs x 3 repeat 3 times non-stop

Hydration

Barbell curls bar x 3 immediately followed by 65lbs x 3 6 sets

Hydration

Neck harness extension/flexion 5lbs x 2 immediately followed by 10lbs x 2 immediately followed by 15lbs x 2 repeat 4 times non-stop

Hydration

Band standing abs light x 5 immediately followed by average x 5 repeat 5 times non-stop

Workout 3

Barbell deadlift 95lbs x 2 immediately followed by 135lbs x 2 repeat 4 times non-stop

Hydration

Sled drag forwards/backwards 95lbs x 10 yards immediately followed by 150lbs x 10 yards repeat 3 times non-stop

Hydration

Kettlebell military press 8kg x 3 immediately followed by 16kg x 3 repeat 3 times non-stop

Hydration

Kettlebell curls 4kg x 2 immediately followed by 6kg x 2 immediately followed by 8kg x 2 repeat 3 times non-stop

Hydration

5 yard dash x 12 times walk back rest only

Kettlebell swings
4kg x 15 reps x 1 set

You will repeat a series of one week phases that require even greater speed and velocity on the movements. Concentrate on firing with as much full body control as possible without sacrificing form or where injury inhibits it.

Phase P2- train 3 times per week for 1 week. Maintain the same weights but improve speed and velocity of movements.

Workout 1

Kettlebell Front squats below parallel box 8kg x 3 immediately followed by 16kg x 3 repeat 3 times non-stop

Hydration

Band good mornings mini-band x 3 immediately followed by monster-mini band x 3 repeat 4 times non-stop

Hydration

Kettlebell farmers walk 12kg x 20 yards immediately followed by 24kg x 2 yards repeat 3 times non-stop

Hydration

Kettlebell shrugs 12kg x 3 immediately followed by 24kg x 3 repeat 3 times non-stop

Hydration

Chins bodyweight x 2 immediately followed by bodyweight plus 20lbs x 2 repeat 3 times non-stop

Hydration

Close grip incline bench 25% of 1rep max x 2 immediately followed by 40% of 1 rep max x 2 repeat 3 times non-stop

Hydration

Kettlebell swings 8kg x 2 immediately followed by 12kg x 2 repeat 3 times non-stop

Workout 2

12 inch step-up with 12kg kettlebells x 3 per leg immediately followed by 16kg x 3 per leg repeat 3 times non-stop

Hydration

Rope sled pulls hand over hand 50lbs x 10 yards immediately followed 100 lbs x 10 yards repeat 3 times non-stop

Hydration

Kettlebell shoulder press 8kg x 3 immediately followed by 12kg x 3 repeat 3 times non-stop

Hydration

Kettlebell curls 4kg x 3 immediately followed by 8kg x 3 repeat 4 times non-stop

Hydration

Band pushdowns light band x 5 immediately followed by average bands x 5 repeat 3 times non-stop

Hydration

Neck harness extension/flexion 15 reps x 2 sets

Hydration

Sport gripper x 3 immediately followed by trainer gripper x 3 repeat 4 times non-stop

Workout 3

Back squat empty bar x 2 immediately followed by 95lbs x 2 repeat 4 times non-stop

Hydration

Kettlebell deadlifts 12kg x 1 immediately followed by 16kg x 1 immediately followed by 24kg x 1 repeat 3 times non-stop

Hydration

Kettlebell bent rows 8kg x 2 immediately followed by 12kg x 2 immediately followed by 16kg x 2 repeat 3 times non-stop

Hydration

Dumbbell hammer curls 4kg x 2 immediately followed by 8kg x 2 repeat 4 times non-stop

Hydration

Sled drags forwards 75lbs x 10 yards immediately followed by 150lbs x 10 yards repeat 2 times non-stop

Hydration

Landmine twist 15lbs x 2 immediately followed by 30lbs x 2 repeat 3 times non-stop

Phase I2- train 3 times per week for 1 week.

Workout 1-

Tire flip- 200lbs x 1 immediately followed by 300lbs x 1 repeat 3 times non-stop

Hydration

Landmine press 25lbs x 1 immediately followed by 50lbs x 1 repeat 3 times non-stop

Hydration

Sled rows 2 plates x 5 immediately followed by 4 plates x 5 repeat 2 times non-stop

Hydration

Sled curls 1 plate x 3 immediately followed by 2 plates x 3 repeat 3 times non-stop

Hydration

Close grip bench press bar x 5 immediately followed by 25% of 1 rep max x 5 immediately followed by 40% 1 rep max x 5 repeat 2 times non-stop

Hydration

Kettlebell swings 4kg x 2 immediately followed by 8kg x 2 immediately followed by 12kg x 2 repeat 3 times non-stop

Workout 2

Trap bar deadlift 95lbs x 2 immediately followed by 135lbs x 2 repeat 4 times non-stop

Hydration

12 inch Step ups 12kg kettlebells x 2 immediately followed by 16kg kettlebells x 2 repeat 3 times non-stop

Hydration

Flat bench 12kg kettlebells x 3 immediately followed by 24kg kettlebells x 3 repeat 3 times non-stop

Hydration

Band triceps pushdowns light x 3 immediately followed by average x 3 repeat 4 times non-stop

Hydration

Band curls light x 3 immediately followed by average x 3 repeat 4 times non-stop

Hydration

Kettlebell swings 4kg x 4 immediately followed by 8kg x 4 repeat 3 times non-stop

Workout 3

Close stance squat bar x 3 immediately followed by 95lbs x 3 repeat 3 times non-stop

Hydration

Kettlebell bent rows 4kg x 3 immediately followed by 8kg x 3 repeat 5 times non-stop

Hydration

Kettlebell shrugs 4kg x 4 immediately followed by 8kg x 4 immediately followed by 12kg x 4 repeat 5 times non-stop

Hydration

Neck harness flexion/extension 5 reps x 5 sets with 5 seconds rest

Phase P3- train 3 times per week for 1 week.

Workout 1

Squat Bar x 25 reps

Bench bar x 25 reps

Bent row bar x 25 reps

Shrug bar x 25 reps

Straight bar curl x 25 reps

Lying triceps extension bar x 25 reps

Workout 2

Bodyweight vertical jumps on soft box 4 inch x 1 immediately followed by 6 inch x 1 repeat 3 times

Hydration

Medicine ball smashes 4 kg x 1 immediately followed by 8kg x 1 immediately followed by 12kg x 1 repeat 4 times

Hydration

Dumbbell Hammer curls 10lbs x 4 immediately followed by 15lbs x 4 immediately followed by 20lbs x 4 repeat 4 times non-stop

Hydration

Neck harness extension/flexion 5lbs x 5 immediately followed by 10lbs x 5 immediately followed by 15lbs x 5 repeat 3 times non-stop

Workout 3

Kettlebell front squats 4kg x 2 immediately followed by 8kg x 2 immediately followed by 12kg x 2 repeat 3 times non-stop

Hydration

Kettlebell clean and jerks 4kg x 2 immediately followed by 8kg x 2 repeat 4 times non-stop

Hydration

Kettlebell snatches 4kg x 2 immediately followed by 8kg x 2 repeat 4 times non-stop

Hydration

Sled push 90lbs x 12 yards immediately followed by 180lbs x 12 yards repeat 3 times non-stop

Hydration

Grippers: perform one rep with each gripper you are capable of closing and repeat from easiest to hardest 3 times

Phase P4- train 3 times per week for 1 week.

Workout 1

Kettlebell farmers walk 16kg x 10 yards immediately followed by 24kg x 10 yards immediately followed by 32kg x 10 yards repeat 2 times non-stop

Hydration

Kettlebell shrugs 16kg x 3 immediately followed by 24kg x 3 immediately followed by 32kg x 3 repeat 3 times non-stop

Hydration

Kettlebell deadlifts 16kg x 3 immediately followed by 24kg x 3 immediately followed by 32kg x 3 repeat 2 times non-stop

Hydration

10 yard sprints x 7 times non-stop walk back rest only

Workout 2

Barbell squat 65lbs x 2 immediately followed by 130lbs x 2 repeat 4 times non-stop

Hydration

Land mine press 15lbs x 2 immediately followed by 30lbs x 2 immediately followed by 45lbs x 2 repeat 2 times non-stop

Hydration

Barbell bent rows 65lbs x 3 immediately followed by 100 lbs x 3 repeat 3 times non-stop

Hydration

Barbell curls bar x 3 immediately followed by 65lbs x 3 6 sets

Hydration

Neck harness extension/flexion 5lbs x 2 immediately followed by 10lbs x 2 immediately followed by 15lbs x 2 repeat 4 times non-stop

Hydration

Band standing abs light x 5 immediately followed by average x 5 repeat 5 times non-stop

Workout 3

Barbell deadlift 95lbs x 2 immediately followed by 135lbs x 2 repeat 4 times non-stop

Hydration

Sled drag forwards/backwards 95lbs x 10 yards immediately followed by 150lbs x 10 yards repeat 3 times non-stop

Hydration

Kettlebell military press 8kg x 3 immediately followed by 16kg x 3 repeat 3 times non-stop

Hydration

Kettlebell curls 4kg x 2 immediately followed by 6kg x 2 immediately followed by 8kg x 2 repeat 3 times non-stop

Hydration

5 yard dash x 12 times walk back rest only

Kettlebell swings
4kg x 15 reps x 1 set

LAW ENFORCEMENT Volume 2.

www.ingramcontent.com/pod-product-compliance
Lightning Source LLC
Chambersburg PA
CBHW081313180526
45170CB00007B/2693

* 9 7 8 0 5 5 7 2 9 4 5 1 0 *